W9-BWY-876

INTRODUCTION

People enjoy keeping pets for the companionship and pleasure they provide. A pet's antics and routines can be fascinating to watch. Children especially develop great pride in their pets and learn about responsibility through caring for them. In addition, breeding small animals like rats is a popular hobby in many parts of the world. Rats even have their own fan clubs, composed of owners who have set up shows and contests for their pets.

The word "rats" spelled backwards

Securely perched on his owner's shoulder, a pet rat checks out the other members of the family menagerie. Rats have become increasingly popular as pets because they are intelligent, interesting little animals that are relatively easy to keep.

is "star." Indeed, a rat is a star pet in many ways. It is gentle and very friendly—even affectionate. A pet rat is not the kind of pet you just look at; rather, it is an interactive pet that thrives on human companionship. A rat likes to play with people and enjoys being taken out of its cage to see and do new things. Pet rats have increased in popularity and acceptance through word of mouth by people who find themselves pleasantly surprised at the friendly, responsive nature of a pet rat.

A pet rat is adaptable, has a good memory, and is extremely intelligent. Many scientists believe the rat is as smart as a dog or a cat. A rat has excellent insight and the ability to solve problems. You can train a pet rat to perform many clever tricks.

This book will describe the basic care of your pet rat. It will also discuss training methods and how to understand rat behavior so that you can train your rat.

This youngster is holding her pet correctly. Young members of the family can enjoy helping to care for a pet rat if they are properly supervised.

RATS IN GENERAL

Scientists refer to rats as successful because of their wide distribution and adaptability. Rats are found all over the world, except on the highest mountains and in the frozen lands near the north and south poles. They adapt well to new situations and have been able to survive massive eradication campaigns. Throughout the centuries, the association of rats with humans has shown that rats are extremely intelligent and resourceful. Rats are cautious, and they have good insight and clever problem-solving ability. These traits have helped the rat persist.

Many rat enthusiasts find exhibition to be the most rewarding part of the hobby. The prize winner shown here is a silver black.

TYPES OF RATS

There are hundreds of different species of rats. One of the more interesting types is the pack rat, or wood rat, of North America. This bushy-tailed rodent resembles a squirrel: it has soft gray fur, large expressive eyes, and a furry tail. This rat is well known for collecting and hoarding objects, especially shiny ones. Another example is the white-throated wood rat, which lives in the desert. It is able to climb cacti without hurting itself. This rat carries spiny needles from the cacti back to its nest to construct a prickly entrance that discourages predators from entering.

Because of pack rats' stockpiling, biologists use pack rat middens (nests) to look for the signs of other animals. Pack rats often add bones and droppings from other animals to their nests. Some pack rat middens are thousands of years old. From these middens, scientists can gain important information about the climate and types of plants that existed long ago.

The most notorious rats are the brown rat *(Rattus norvegicus)* and the black rat, also called roof rat *(Rattus rattus)*, both of which occur worldwide. The brown rat is larger than the black rat. It is most often associated with people and their buildings. The brown rat lives on the ground, usually in underground burrows,

A rat is a very active animal and will enjoy the opportunity to be let out of its cage for exercise.

RATS AND PEOPLE

Long ago, even before the beginning of recorded history, brown and black rats found advantages in living with people. Bones of both types of rats have been found in Stone Age dwellings. Rats could live more comfortably with people in their cities and farms than in the wild.

The brown and black rats migrated along trade and military routes. The rats did not walk; they cleverly hitched rides in containers of food, in horse-drawn carts, or in ships that they entered by climbing up docking ropes. Thus the rat travelled wherever people went.

With the rats came their fleas. Wild rats harbor fleas that carry the disease-causing organism for bubonic plague. Scholars have attributed more than one hundred plagues to rats over the last two thousand years. The great ratborne plagues changed the course of human history. For example, the Great Black Death of the Middle Ages killed more than 75 million people worldwide. In Europe, the loss of 25 million people contributed to the end of the feudal system. Serfs, who had once been cheap labor, became in short supply and more able to collectively bargain with landowners.

Success in controlling seafaring rats is one of the main reasons for the decline in ratborne epidemics such as bubonic plague. Not only do modern ships have rat guards, but they also are actively inspected for rats. If any rats are found, the ship is fumigated.

and prefers wet areas. Black rats are good climbers and are also found in buildings, but usually in the upstairs part. Black rats prefer to live in wooden buildings because of their climbing habits. Both of these species originated in the temperate regions of southeastern Asia. The black rat migrated west from Asia first, but the more aggressive brown rat has replaced it in many places.

Besides spreading disease, rats cause enormous damage to people's food supplies every year. Rats destroy food by eating it, gnawing it, or contaminating it with their droppings. For example, rats often take a bite out of one potato before moving on to take a bite out of another, thus making each unfit to consume. In addition, rats are destructive to buildings, and by gnawing through electrical wires they can cause fires.

Rats have cohabited with humans for so long that it is not surprising that their presence is incorporated into our expressions, our literature, and even our movies. There are a wealth of expressions that use the rat, such as "You dirty rat" and "fight like a cornered rat." These expressions usually depict the rat as vicious or destructive, in contrast to those that portray mice as shy and timid (e.g., "meek as a mouse"). Rats have figured prominently in many stories, notably the story of the Pied Piper of Hamelin in Germany. Rats starred in two popular horror films in the early 1970s (*Willard* and its sequel *Ben*). In some cultures, the rat has been considered a symbol of good luck (e.g., China), whereas medieval Europeans believed the rat was evil.

People have eaten rats in many parts of the world since ancient times. Rats have been an important staple of food during famines, being sold in markets just like any other item. They are still an important source of nutrition and are widely eaten

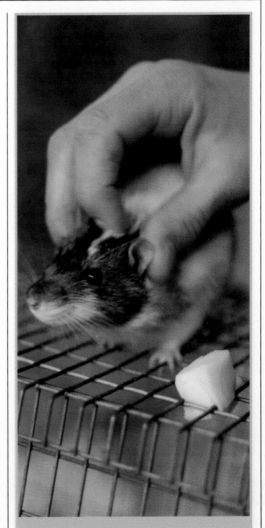

This rat particularly likes to be scratched behind the ears. Regularly spending time with your pet will strengthen the pet-owner bond.

today. For example, the greater cane rat is eaten in Africa, and the rice rat is eaten in Thailand. One restaurant in Guangzhou, China specializes in serving rat in at least thirty different ways.

It is believed that rats were first domesticated in the early 1800s for use in ratting contests with dogs, usually terrier breeds. The object of these contests was to have a dog kill the largest number of rats in a given time. The albino rat was first popularized in these ratting contests because blood showed up better on its fur. By the late eighteenth century, rats were being used for scientific studies.

RATS IN THE LABORATORY

The most commonly used modern laboratory rat is a descendant of the brown rat. Breeding rats for scientific purposes began in 1906 at Philadelphia's Wistar Institute. There are some strains of rats still called Wistars. Different strains of rats often look physically different from one another. For example, the Sprague-Dawley albino has a narrow head and a tail longer than its body, whereas the Wistar albino has a wide head and shorter tail. The Long-Evans strain is the well-known hooded rat. It is smaller than many albino strains. The hooded rat was developed by two scientists, Dr. Long and Dr. Evans, in 1915 at the University of California.

Scientists have bred different strains of rats to be genetically resistant or susceptible to various conditions (e.g., hypertension, diabetes, or obesity). Unless you know the strain of rat and what it is prone to, you usually cannot recognize a rat with a predisposed genetic trait. Some types of rats used in research are barrier-raised in specific pathogen-free colonies (abbreviated SPF). This means that the rats are disease-free. These rats are born by Caesarean section to prevent contamination with germs, and barriers are used as additional precautions. The barriers are elaborate sterile procedures and conditions that protect and maintain the rats' germ-free status and thus their value in scientific studies.

Research with laboratory rats has contributed to many medical breakthroughs. Millions of rats are used by scientists each year in research and testing. The rats are used in studies on aging, drug effects, vitamin effects, behavior, alcoholism, arthritis, hypertension, and infectious diseases, to list just a few. These studies have helped scientists to discover the cause of diseases, understand how a disease affects the body, and provide better cures for many diseases.

SENSES AND SKILLS

Rats have some acute senses that help them to survive. They are nocturnal animals and are most active at night. Their vision is poor; they see in various shades of gray and can see well only up close. They have special night vision, however, which enables them to recognize motion up to thirty feet away and to identify shapes in dim light. As you might suspect, the albino rat's red eyes are more sensitive to light than their dark-eyed counterparts.

Rats use their whiskers to help them sense their environment. The whiskers that are found near the eyes, lips, and cheeks greatly aid the rat in its wanderings. When the rat is running along, the whiskers on the cheeks perceive the horizontal and ground surfaces, while the ones above the eyes detect overhead surfaces.

Rats have an acute sense of hearing. They can recognize noises and locate them to within half a foot. They cannot hear low notes, but they can perceive shrill notes that are too high for humans to hear. Their excellent sense of smell helps them locate food and find other rats.

shyness" contributes to the rats' resiliency and the difficulty in trying to eliminate them by feeding them poisoned food.

A rat has two pairs of chisel-like incisors in the front of its mouth. These teeth never stop growing and can grow up to five inches a year. A rat's teeth are constantly worn down by its gnawing and

There are hundreds of species of rats. Included among them is the pack rat, which is shown here. This specimen was captured in the wild by scientists.

Rats have a highly developed sense of taste, which helps them detect minute quantities of poisonous or unpleasant substances. Rats get sick from poisonous or bad food because they cannot vomit. Those that survive a single episode of poisoning usually reject any food with the same taste as that which made them sick. This "bait

chewing on hard substances. Rats have powerful jaw muscles and teeth. They can gnaw through the hard outer shell of a nut or even lead pipes. Their 12 rear molars are used for grinding food. The space between the incisors and the rear molars is called the diastema. When a rat eats, its cheeks block this space to prevent any sharp food from being swallowed.

These children are letting their pets get acquainted. Pet ownership can help to foster a child's sense of responsibility.

A rat's tail is covered with overlapping scales that have three hairs projecting from under the edge of each scale. The surface is covered with an orange-yellow wax. The rat's tail helps it balance when it climbs. The scales can ruffle backward and give the rat a good grip. The rat lacks sweat glands but uses its tail as a thermoregulating device. The rat can regulate its body temperature by constricting the blood vessels in its tail to conserve heat, or it can radiate heat from these same vessels to cool off.

A healthy young rat usually carries its tail in the air to help its balance, but an old or sick rat might drag its tail. Many people do not like the appearance of a rat's tail. If a pet rat's tail were fuzzy like a gerbil's, rats would probably be even more popular as pets.

Rats have an array of survival skills. A rat can run at a top speed of six miles an hour and jump upward three feet. A cornered rat does not always surrender; it might attack its pursuer even if it is a dog, a cat, or a person. Rats are excellent swimmers. They can swim as far as half a mile in the open sea and tread water for three days. They can also swim underwater. Rats have even been found swimming at sea several days after the ship they were on sank.

Rats communicate with other rats through body language. For example, a rat that wants to be groomed will crouch in front of another rat, and a rat that challenges another rat will assume a threatening stance. Rats also communicate with one another through pheromones. Pheromones are chemicals secreted from the body that facilitate communication and influence behavior between members of the same species. An example of this is territorial urine-marking. Male rats, in particular, mark their territory with urine. Other rats will avoid the marked area. Unlike other animals, which have special scent glands for pheromones, the source of rat pheromones might be in their urine, droppings, or skin, because rats do not have scent glands.

Rats that live within a colony have an established social order. The dominant rats are those that win fights and get the best food. A rat fight is an amazing sight. The rats' bodies get stiff, and their hairs stand on end. They grind their teeth and wag their tails. A rat leaps, pushes, boxes, and bites its opponent. It appears that a rat's low social status can be passed on to future generations. These weaker rats get less food, so their young do not grow as fast or as big as the offspring of dominant rats.

Rats are exceptional animals. They continue to prevail against attempts to exterminate them and even win grudging respect for their resourcefulness from professional exterminators. The same qualities that make them such skillful and versatile adversaries of people in the wild help make rats marvelous pets.

RATS AS PETS

Some pet rat owners refer to rats as "superpets" because of their superb pet qualities. Pet rats are friendly and curious. They are extremely intelligent and enjoy human company. They make good pets for anyone of almost any age. When your pet hears you come home, it will greet you at the cage door,

classroom pets. They are not timid like mice, and unlike hamsters, rats rarely bite.

Domestic rats have been raised in captivity for more than a century. They bear little resemblance to their wild ancestors. A pet rat is very clean, performing an elaborate grooming ritual several times a day. The rat first licks its front

A winning silver fawn rat.

waiting to come out and play. A pet rat is a true companion. You can let it ride on your shoulder, carry it in a pocket, or tuck it in your sleeve. Your pet rat will learn its name and can be trained to come to you when called. Many children are introduced to rats as pets at school. Rats make excellent

feet, or "hands." Then, using both hands, it washes its face and behind its ears. It cleans the fur all over its body and also licks its hind toes after scratching with them. You will also see your pet clean its long tail. A rat is very fastidious and will even set up a separate toilet area in its cage.

HOW TO CHOOSE A RAT

You can buy a rat from a pet shop. Be certain that your rat comes from a clean, uncrowded cage. Rats that come from a dirty, crowded environment are less likely to make good pets. Crowded animals are more likely to be aggressive toward one another and have lowered resistance to infectious diseases. Choose a young rat four to eight weeks old (about four to eight inches long). A young rat tames quickly and makes a better pet than an older one.

Carefully examine the rat you are buying for signs of poor health. A healthy rat has a smooth, shiny coat and clear eyes, and it feels solid. Watch out for animals that have dull, fluffy coats, bald patches, runny eyes or noses, wounds, or lumps; also avoid those that are listless or feel frail. It is important to listen to the breathing of the rat. Do not buy a rat that wheezes or sneezes. Additionally, if you are interested in a rat that does not exhibit either of these symptoms but is caged with other rats who *are* wheezing and sneezing, do not purchase the animal. Such sounds indicate a contagious (among rats) respiratory disease. If possible, you should check the rat's front teeth to make sure they meet properly.

Young rats should be curious and playful and investigate a hand that is put into their cage. A good choice is a rat that feels relaxed when held. A frightened rat is stiff, and its nails feel sharp on your skin. If the rat doesn't calm down after being held awhile, choose another.

Rats come in a variety of fancy colors, markings, and coat types. Some of the colors include white, black, lilac, champagne, apricot, Himalayan, agouti, pearl, and cinnamon pearl. Their eyes can be red or black, depending on their coloring.

Some of the more common marked varieties include hooded, capped, variegated, Berkshire, and Irish. Hooded rats have a colored hood (e.g., black or cream) that covers their head and shoulders and continues in a saddle down the spine to the tail. Capped rats have a colored head but not a colored saddle. They have a white blaze or spot on the face, and the rest of their body is white. Variegated rats have colored heads and shoulders and a white blaze on the forehead. The variegated (or mixed) markings cover the body from the shoulders to the tail, although the belly color is white. The markings of a Berkshire rat are symmetrical, with a white chest, belly, and feet. There is a white spot on the forehead. The body markings of the Irish rat are similar to those of Berkshire, except that the Irish has a white equilateral triangle on the chest and does not have a white belly.

Most rats have a smooth coat, but there are exceptions. The Rex has a curly coat and curly whiskers. The velour has a coat that is the texture of crushed velour. The Sphynx is hairless.

MALE OR FEMALE?

Should you get a male or female rat? If you want to breed

rats, you will need to purchase a female. Female rats are smaller and sleeker than male rats and tend to be more active. Male rats are more likely to sit contentedly in your lap while you tickle behind their ears. Both sexes make excellent pets, but males are more likely to urine-mark.

It is easiest to determine the

HOW MANY?

In nature, rats are social animals, living in family groups or colonies with a dominance hierarchy. Therefore some people believe that a rat is happiest when kept with another rat. However, it should not be considered necessary to keep rats together. A single rat might be more

This rat and cat have spent several years together in the same household and tolerate each other's presence. However, it should be noted that such a relationship is the exception rather than the rule. Use caution when exposing your rat to *any* other pets that you may have.

sex of young rats by comparing them to their cagemates. Generally, the distance between the anus and the genital papilla will be fifty percent greater in males. You might also notice a slight swelling where the male's scrotum will be. If you hold the rat upright, the testes will descend; and you will be able to see that it is a male.

responsive and friendly because you are its only playmate.

If you decide to get two rats, you will need to purchase a larger cage, and you will need to clean it more often. Make sure the rats are the same sex unless you want one or more litters of rat babies. Your two rats will groom each other, play-fight, and sleep curled up with one another.

You must be careful if you decide to get your older rat a companion. The older rat might resent the introduction of the new rat in its territory. The two rats might fight, and the newcomer will be at a disadvantage. If you must break up a rat fight, use a towel to separate the fighting rats. Place each rat in a separate cage so that each can tend to any wounds that it may have. You can apply an antibiotic ointment to any bad cuts. Prevent rat fights by keeping apart any rats that appear to dislike each other.

Many pet owners quarantine new arrivals. If you purchase rats at different times, you might want to isolate them in another room for approximately two weeks. This allows you enough time to be sure they are not sick and helps to avoid infecting your other rats if they are.

Your rat cannot become friends with hamsters, gerbils, mice, birds, or other small animals. They will fight, and the rat will probably kill the other animal. Rats can become friendly with larger animals such as rabbits, and with some dogs and cats. Proceed with caution when introducing your pet to another animal. It is probably best not to introduce your rat to any of the terrier breeds of dog, because they were bred as ratters.

Make sure your rat can't climb onto any fish tank that you might have. Your rat instinctively knows how to fish. It will search the water using a sweeping motion with its paws. Any curious fish that comes to investigate is likely to be caught by your rat!

If you keep your rat in an aquarium, use a screen cover to keep your rat in, and other pets out! Photo courtesy of Four Paws.

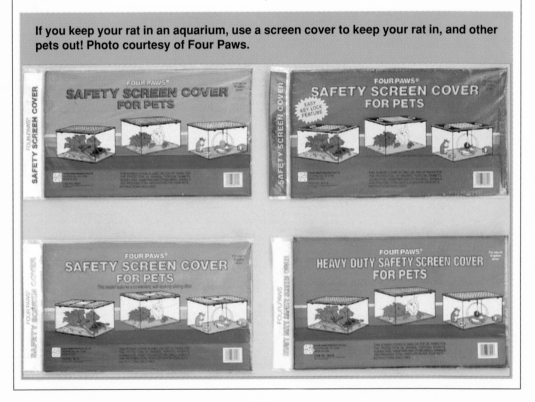

HOUSING

Pet shops offer a wide variety of suitable cages for your rat. You can select from all-metal wire-frame cages, bird cages made of hard plastic and wire, or glass aquariums. A cage that measures 20 in. long by 10 in. wide by 12 in. high is ideal for your pet rat. If you house more than one rat together in the same cage or intend to breed rats, you should buy a larger cage. Cages designed for hamsters and mice are generally not large enough for your rat. Rats are active animals and do best in a roomy cage.

If you buy a wire-frame cage, make sure the space between the bars is not larger than $^1/_2$ in.; if it is, your rat might be able to squeeze out. Typical rat mesh is two wires per inch. If you intend to breed your rat, make sure the space between the wires is not larger than this or the babies might fall or crawl out. There is usually no problem with a rat's getting its foot caught in the wire-mesh bottom of a commercially made cage, especially if you pile bedding all over the mesh floor. If your cage has a wire shelf, you might cover it with a wire mesh that measures $^1/_2$ in. by $^1/_2$ in.; This will help to prevent your pet from getting its foot caught (and possibly broken). A well-made wire cage should have a tray bottom that slides out for easy cleaning, or the wire-frame cage should lift off the bottom tray.

Sometimes shavings or food might spill out of your pet's wire-frame cage, or your rat might even kick them out. In such cases, you can purchase clear plastic sheeting or seed guards in the bird section of a pet store to put around the base of the cage. You can also use a fine-screen wire mesh. Another option is to place the cage on an attractive piece of material, which will at least keep any spills directly off the floor.

Some wire-frame cages might come with an exercise wheel. Make sure the wheel is sized for rats (e.g., 12 in. to 14 in. in diameter), not hamsters. However, many grown rats do not like to use an exercise wheel. You might wish to replace the wheel with another toy.

A bird cage of the size suggested for rats makes a good home for your pet rat. The cage will have a slide-out plastic tray that is easy to wash and clean. A bird cage is tall and provides vertical room in which your rat can play. You can encourage your rat to make use of the height by setting up bird perches and adding ladders, platforms, and parrot swings. Be sure to buy door clips, because many rats learn to open the door of a bird cage.

A glass aquarium is another good choice for your rat's home. They come in many sizes, are easy to clean, and offer a good view of your pet. You will need to buy a screen cover and clips for the aquarium unless you can make a cover out of sturdy wire mesh. You need to cover the aquarium because your rat can jump as high as three feet! Aquariums also have the advantage of preventing bedding and food from being kicked out by your active rat.

Molded acrylic aquariums also can be used to house your pet rat. These aquariums are lightweight and will not break, but they can tend to become scratched, which can make it harder to see your pet. They also are more expensive than glass aquariums.

While it can be fun to construct your own cage, it is simpler and cheaper to just buy one. Cages made of wood are difficult to keep clean because they tend to absorb urine and odors.

BEDDING

Bedding keeps your pet warm and clean and helps to deodorize the cage. There are many kinds of bedding available, such as ground corn cobs and peanut shells. Wood shavings make an excellent bedding material. Rats seem to prefer shavings. They can burrow into the shavings and it's easier to make nests in the shavings. Fluffy shavings will absorb better than those that are coarsely ground. Shavings should be dust-free to avoid irritation to your pet's respiratory tract. Be wary of using sawdust, which can be too dusty.

There are many different types of wood shavings available at your pet shop. Pine shavings are widely available and usually inexpensive. Chlorophyll shavings are usually dyed green and are good deodorizers. They are more expensive than plain pine.

Cedar shavings are excellent deodorizers but are even more expensive. They can cause and aggravate respiratory distress in some rats. Additionally, cedar shavings are not used for rats in laboratory studies. The shavings contain certain chemicals that can cause an increase in the production of liver enzymes. This increase can affect the results of laboratory tests. You should not worry about the adverse effect of an over-production of liver enzymes in your pet rat, especially if you mix only small amounts of cedar shavings with pine shavings. Nonetheless, because of these possible side effects, it is often best not to use any cedar shavings at all.

Whatever type of housing you choose, make sure that it is large enough to comfortably accommodate your pet and cage accessories such as toys, food bowl, and water bottle.

You can also add alfalfa, which is available at pet stores that sell guinea pigs and rabbits, to your pet's cage. It is not absorbent, but it has a pleasant fragrance. Your pet will enjoy tunneling through it and might nibble some.

ACCESSORIES

Your rat needs a nesting box for security and sleeping. Always call your pet out of its box; don't reach in and pull it out. The nesting box is your rat's private retreat. A nesting box can be made from the bottom part of an empty (washed and dried) half-gallon milk carton or part of an empty cereal box. The nesting box will need to be replaced every few weeks. You can give your rat an old sock, a piece of an old shirt, or unscented tissue to put into its box. If you use a sock or shirt, be sure to wash it at least once a week so that it stays clean-smelling.

Provide your rat with fresh water, using a gravity-fed water bottle available in pet stores. The best models are made of plastic and have a metal spout. A special holder, also available at pet stores, enables you to hang the water bottle in an aquarium. Your rat will drink about an ounce of water a day. Do *not* use an open dish to provide your rat with water. Your rat will fill the dish with its bedding and food, and the water will become unsanitary.

Place your rat's food in a dish. If you have a metal cage, you can attach the dish to the side to prevent it from being knocked over. If you use a free-standing dish, make sure it is heavy enough that your rat cannot tip it. Pet stores sell a variety of ceramic dishes in attractive colors; they are ideal. Use a separate container for any moist foods that you feed your pet.

These weanling rats are ready to go to new homes. If you are keeping several rats together, you will have to devote extra time to cage cleaning and maintenance.

Your rat will play on almost anything you put into its cage. If you hang a large wood-and-rock toy (specially made for parrots) in your pet's cage, you might see him swing from it and gnaw on the wood. Ladders, bells, small balls, and swings can all be used in your pet's cage to make it more interesting. In general, many of the toys made for parrots can safely be used in your rat's cage, and your rat will enjoy them. Your rat needs to chew, but be aware that wooden toys might pick up

The Nylabone Company produces a wide variety of chew products that are suitable for rats.

odor. You might wish to use some plastic toys when possible, because they are easier to keep clean.

Researchers have found that rats raised together in spacious cages with toys to play with and mazes to run through were more intelligent than rats raised alone in cages containing just food and nests. These results suggest that if your rat is stimulated with toys and activities, it might become smarter.

WHERE TO KEEP THE CAGE

You should keep your pet's cage in a draft-free area out of direct sunlight. Do not place the cage near a heater or air conditioner vent or in front of a window. Don't leave any items like clothing or papers next to your pet's cage, because your rat will pull them into the cage and chew them. Place your pet's cage where you can get maximum benefit from it. You can rest the cage on a stand or on a table. If you place the cage on the floor, you can arrange an attractive piece of material underneath it. You should make the cage a pleasant and intriguing part of a room.

Your rat can be kept outdoors if the temperature does not drop below 40°F (4°C). However, you will probably enjoy your pet more if you keep its cage inside your house. Pet rats don't have any objectionable odor the way mice do. In fact, some people think rats smell pleasantly of sandalwood. Your rat's home will smell only if you don't clean if often enough. Protect your rat from other household pets that could hurt it. This means making sure the door to its cage is closed, and it might even mean closing the door to the room where you keep your pet.

CLEANING

A clean cage plays an important role in keeping your rat healthy. Clean your pet's cage at least once a week. Don't just put in new

ROAR-HIDE™, by the makers of Nylabone, is the longest lasting yet completely edible form of rawhide available. Nylabone® products can be purchased in pet shops.

bedding over the old; replace *all* the bedding, even if it doesn't look dirty. If your pet's home is an aquarium, you can use a cat litter scooper to scoop out the shavings. Be sure to remove any old food your rat might have hidden away. Always keep the water bottle clean. The inside of the bottle and the tube will probably feel slimy, even if they look clean. You can purchase a slender bristle brush (of the type used to clean filter systems) from the fish section of a pet store to help you clean your rat's water bottle. Check that no shavings or food are in the tube. Also clean your pet's food dish and toys.

Your rat will establish a toilet area in one corner of the cage. You can clean out this area approximately every four days to help keep your pet's home odor-free. If you clean it too often, your rat will not be able to establish the area. Chlorophyll or cedar shavings in this area will

A typically alert pet rat enjoys the view from the top of its cage.

A gravity-fed water bottle, which can be suspended from the side of the housing unit, is the best way to provide your rat with water. It will ensure that the water supply is sanitary and uncontaminated by food particles and bits of bedding.

also help control any odors.

Once a month, do a thorough cleaning. Disinfect the cage and the surrounding area. Pet stores sell mild cleansers that are safe for animals. Scrape off or file off any grime that might have accumulated on the wires of the cage.

Cage-cleaning time doesn't have to be drudgery. You can let your rat ride around on your shoulder or play in the room while you clean its quarters. If you don't want to play with your pet at this time, you can also place it into a carrying cage or a tall covered bucket.

FEEDING

Just like people, rats are omnivorous. This means that they eat fruits and vegetables, grains, seeds, nuts, and meats. Your pet will probably eat almost anything you feed it. It is important, however, to provide your pet with a balanced and nutritious diet. Nutrition is a key factor in promoting good health and a long life.

It is important that the food you feed your rat is fresh. Food that is old can become stale and lose some of its nutritional value. Do not buy large quantities of food, because it will take too long a time to use all of it. Check to see whether there is an expiration date on the package of food. Store your pet's food in an airtight container, such as a glass jar with a lid. This will help keep it fresh and prevent spoilage.

A balanced diet includes the correct amounts of quality protein, fat, carbohydrates, vitamins, and minerals. All these nutrients interact in the building, maintenance, and functioning of your pet's body. It is also important to feed a diet that does not include too much of these nutrients. For example, some rats are susceptible to kidney failure (called chronic renal failure). This condition can be brought on and aggravated by feeding a diet that has too much protein.

The amount of protein that your pet needs is influenced by a number of physiological factors, such as age and reproductive status. Male rats and nonbreeding females older than three months need less protein than when they are in their most active growth period. Pregnant or nursing rats require increased protein. A good diet for rats should contain approximately 14 percent protein.

Good sources of protein for your rat can come from both animal and plant sources. Different sources of protein vary in their digestibility, that is, how much of the protein can be used by your pet. For example, feathers and hair are high in protein, but this protein is not easily digested and used by your pet. Chicken meat, on the other hand, contains high-quality protein that is more easily digested than either feathers or hair. Convenient protein sources are dry dog kibble (use the low-protein, low-fat type made for older or overweight dogs), hard-boiled eggs, rolled oats, sunflower seeds, canary seed, buckwheat, linseed, and millet. Avoid feeding dry cat food, which is too high in protein and fat.

Fats are a significant source of calories and energy. They make up part of the structure of every cell and are necessary for absorption of fat-soluble vitamins (i.e., vitamins A, D, E, and K). Fats help to prevent and alleviate skin problems. A deficiency of fat can show up as scaly skin, or rough, thin hair. Rats do well on diets containing approximately five percent fat. Just as in people, a diet high in fat is associated with obesity and decreased life span.

Providing a well-rounded diet for a rat is not difficult, as rats will eat a wide variety of foods.

Carbohydrates are used as a source of energy. Your pet will easily get enough carbohydrates with a diet based on seeds and cereal grains. For example, most grains and seeds are at least fifty percent carbohydrate.

VITAMINS AND MINERALS

Vitamins are necessary as catalysts for chemical reactions in the body. They are absorbed in the rat's upper small intestine. A number of vitamins are synthesized in rats by intestinal bacteria. They include folic acid, biotin, riboflavin, and vitamins B_{12} and K. They are absorbed in the ileum. These vitamins are available to rats by means of coprophagy: the eating of special droppings that contain the vitamins synethesized by the bacteria. If you have a wire-frame cage, make sure the bedding covers the mesh floor of the cage so that these droppings are within reach of your pet. Rats that are bred to be germ-free for use in research cannot synthesize these vitamins since they lack the bacteria. Therefore, the vitamins must be supplied in their diet.

Knowledge of bacteria-synthesized vitamins has been used to make a more effective rat-killing poison. Warfarin is a rat poison that interferes with normal blood clotting. A rat that eats this poison will die of internal bleeding. However, some rats have become more resistant to the effects of warfarin. Vitamin K is a catalyst that is necessary for the normal blood clotting process. When sulfa drugs (antibiotics) are added to warfarin, the bacteria that synthesize vitamin K are killed. The rat then lacks an essential ingredient for blood clotting and is less able to resist the effects of the poison.

A vitamin deficiency in your rat can cause specific symptoms, such as sterility in male rats fed a diet low in Vitamin E. But usually there is more than one symptom of a vitamin deficiency because various nutrients interact; a diet deficient in one vitamin is likely to be deficient in others as well.

Rats require minerals and trace elements, such as iron, magnesium, calcium, phosphate, iodine, zinc, and copper. Minerals have many functions, from the structural role of calcium and phosphate in bones to the role of iron in bringing oxygen to the body. You can see what percentage of minerals is contained in some pre-packaged pet foods by looking at the percentage of ash (ash is primarily minerals) listed under the guaranteed analysis. Of course, the percentage doesn't tell you exactly which minerals are present or in what amounts.

Feeding your pet a fresh, high-quality diet will usually ensure adequate intake of needed vitamins and minerals. However, you can buy a vitamin-and-mineral supplement for small animals at most pet stores. Liquid supplements can be mixed in with your pet's drinking water. Be sure to change the water frequently. Some rats might not like the taste of the water with the supplement in it. You can try letting your pet lick the suggested dosage off the dropper or putting the liquid on a piece of bread or dog food. Powdered supplements can be mixed with the dry food. A small drop of vegetable oil can be used so that the powder sticks to the food. Vitamin and mineral supplements are also available as pellets. Do not give your pet more of the supplement than is recommended on the label directions. Remember, a vitamin and mineral supplement will not necessarily improve a poor-quality diet.

SUGGESTED DIETS

You can feed your pet food pellets made especially for rats. These pellets contain a balance of all the nutrients your pet needs. Breeders of large numbers of animals often use these pellets because they are convenient and easy to feed. If you choose to feed your pet only these pellets, you can supplement them with a fresh fruit and vegetable mixture.

You can use pre-mixed foods for hamsters or gerbils as the basis for your rat's diet. These mixes

This rat is receiving a treat after successfully making its way through a maze. Keep treat portions small to prevent your rat from becoming overweight.

contain seeds, grains, nuts, alfalfa pellets, and sometimes dry kibble. You will find that your pet has a preference for certain items in the mix but will not eat others, such as the alfalfa pellets. The variety of the mix can be increased by adding different kinds of bird seed (such as wild bird, parakeet, canary, or finch mix) and dry unsweetened cereals found in your home.

You can create your own mix of food to feed your pet. Pet stores often sell grains and seeds in bulk, which you can buy by the pound. You can blend together grains such as rolled oats, wheat, and cracked corn, and add bird seed, such as wild bird mix, parakeet mix, finch mix, and so forth. Some parrot mixes contain a high percentage of high-fat, high-protein seeds, such as sunflower and safflower seeds, and peanuts. You should use a proportionately smaller amount of this mix in your blend. You can add a small amount of dry dog kibble and some dry unsweetened cereals to complete the mix.

In addition to grains and seeds, you should feed your pet a mixture of fruits and vegetables. You can make a mixture from the foods you have in your house (e.g., grated carrots, spinach, strawberries, bananas, apples, diced cucumber, corn, raisins, and cooked potato). Be sure to wash and dry the food. Make no more than five days' worth and store in an airtight container in your refrigerator. Use a separate dish to feed your pet any moist foods.

Start by feeding your pet a small amount (no more than one teaspoon) of the fruit and vegetable mix. Do not feed so much that there are leftovers in the cage. Observe your rat's desire for the fruits and vegetables, and use this experience to determine how much to feed. It is very important to remove any uneaten moist food. Moist food left in the cage can become putrid. Bacteria can grow on it, which could make your pet sick. Fruits and vegetables are an important supplement that can help alleviate any dietary deficiencies. Rats fed fruits and vegetables seem to have a lower incidence of some illnesses, especially skin ailments.

TREATS

Your pet will greet with delight any treats that you give it. Treats can include table scraps such as cornbread or a portion of potato with skin on it. Rats will also enjoy items such as rice, soup, or a small piece of sandwich. Put any table scraps in the dish for moist foods. Remember to remove any uneaten moist foods, or feed only as much as your rat will eat in one sitting.

You will find that your pet likes foods that are the least good for it. Such foods include sweet, salty, and fatty foods. Treats such as crackers, cookies and chips should be fed rarely, if at all. (An exception to this rule can be made for rat-training sessions, but it is still best to try to use healthy foods for treats—if your pet will accept them.)

Pet stores sell plenty of goodies that you can give your rat. Practically any treat sold for other animals will be appreciated by your pet. For example, egg biscuit (sold for birds) is relished by pet rats, as are honey-coated seed sticks, which can be hung in your pet's cage.

Your rat will even enjoy eating insects. Mealworms are a nice treat for your rat and can be bought at most pet stores. Most rats will readily eat grasshoppers, moths, and some caterpillars. However, some rats are afraid of insects, and some insects have formidable defenses (including stinging hairs and sharp claws). In general, if you can handle the insect without discomfort, your rat can too. Be sure to catch insects from areas that you know have *not* been treated with insecticides or herbicides.

Your pet's teeth are constantly growing, but so slowly that you cannot notice it. The teeth have to continue growing because otherwise, when your rat chews and gnaws on hard foods and other objects, the teeth would wear away. You can provide your rat with hard foods to gnaw on, such as nuts in their shells, dry macaroni, and artificial dog bones (flavored nylon bones work well). If you give your rat hard foods in its regular diet, long teeth should not be a problem.

HOW MUCH TO FEED

How much your rat needs to eat will change throughout its life. You will need to feed your rat enough food to meet its energy needs. The amount will vary not only upon age and reproductive status but also upon activity level. A rat that is allowed to run around and play with you will require more food than one that just sits in its cage. Even the environment and time of day

Fruits are a good supplement to a rat's basic diet. Be sure to thoroughly wash them before feeding them to your pet.

can affect your pet's appetite. For example, it will eat less food during the day than at night, and it will eat less when it is hot.

It is best to feed your rat the same amount of food at the same time each day. Since your rat is nocturnal and most active at night, you should feed it in the evening rather than in the morning. Always have some kind of food available in your pet's food dish. An adult rat can eat approximately 15 to 20 grams ($^1/_2$ to $^3/_4$ oz.) of food a day. Exactly how much depends on the kind of food being fed. Feeding your pet $^1/_3$ cup of grain and seed mixture is a good start. The amount you feed should be adjusted according to your observations. You want to feed your pet enough food for it to maintain a stable weight. Your pet should feel solid and sleek without any extra folds of fat. Any marked loss or increase in your rat's appetite could signal an illness.

Young rats begin to eat solid food when they are about 2 $^1/_2$ weeks old. They have large appetites and should be free-fed, that is, given all the food they can eat. By four months of age, a rat's growth will have slowed considerably. You should then stabilize the amount of food you give it. A female rat's energy requirements increase during pregnancy and increase even more during nursing. A pregnant or lactating rat should also be free-fed.

A rat bite is a rare occurrence. However, there are two food-related reasons that your pet might grab at a finger (usually lightly, at that). First, if your rat smells food on your hand, it might mistakenly nibble your finger. Prevention is clear and easy. Wash your hands before handling your

NUTRITION EXPERIMENTS

The rat is used in many experiments on nutrition. These experiments provide useful and important information. You might be interested to learn that scientists have found that the amount, composition, and type of calories in food can affect a rat's lifespan. For example, it is widely known among scientists that long-term calorie restriction (sixty

Rat bites are not common. However, your pet might nip your finger if it smells of food. To prevent this, wash your hands before handling your rat.

rat if you have been eating with them (e.g., chicken or corn) or if you have been preparing any food. Second, it is best not to feed your pet through the wires of its cage. If you do, your rat might think that you have food for it when you don't, and it will grab anything you put through the wires, even your finger. Always open the cage door to give your pet its food.

percent of the mean food intake of free-fed rats) extends the lifespan and slows age-related diseases in rats. It has also been found that rats fed high-protein diets do not live as long as those that are maintained on low-protein diets. Other studies have shown that rats live longer if they are fed a high-fiber, low-protein, and low-fat diet. In addition, female rats fed high-fiber, low-fat diets might have a reduced incidence of mammary tumors.

The results of these studies show that diet plays an important role in the health and longevity of rats. It is not recommended that you try to specifically apply such results when feeding your pet rat, especially food restriction. You must remember that the scientists who conduct such studies use controlled conditions, highly specific diets, and distinct strains of rats. It is not possible for you to replicate their results with your pet rat. You can, however, keep the results in mind when feeding your pet. For example, do not overfeed your rat, especially a rich diet high in fat and protein. And, by feeding your pet a fruit and vegetable mixture, you will ensure that it gets plenty of fiber.

Rats are very intelligent animals and quickly respond to people and things in their environment.

With patience and persistence, these youngsters trained their pets to go through a maze. Mazes are just one of a number of devices that can be implemented in a training program.

TAMING

Before you bring your new pet home, ask for a small handful of the shavings from the rat's cage to put into its new home. The smell of its old cage will comfort your pet and help it adjust in its new home. Once home, let your pet get used to its new cage and surroundings before you play with it. In many cases, a rat is immediately comfortable and will respond well to your friendly attempts. After a few hours, you can usually take your pet out of its cage. Timid rats are unusual, but if your pet seems shy or nervous, leave it alone for awhile, or talk soothingly to it. Partially covering the cage with a cloth will help give your rat a feeling of security and make it feel less vulnerable.

You need to decide on a name for your pet to help you tame and train it. Your rat will come to associate hearing its name with feeding time, a scratch behind its ears, exploration, and playtime.

Besides using its name, you should also think of another way to get your pet's attention. A clicking noise made with your tongue, "tch-tch," or a soft whistle are examples. A vibration also helps to get its attention (e.g., tapping lightly on the floor with your fingers). Whenever you feed your pet, take it out to play, or just greet it in its cage, use its name and the attention-getting signal that you have selected.

Always use two hands when holding your rat. This will help your rat to feel more secure and will lessen the chances of any accidental injuries.

HOLDING AND CARRYING YOUR RAT

When you pick up your pet, scoop your hand underneath its belly and let it rest its front and hind paws on your hand. If it is too big for one of your hands, use both. When you *hold* your rat, always use two hands. One hand should support the front legs and shoulders, and the other should cradle the hind legs. Snuggle your pet against your body for greater security. Rats are docile when held and will not jump out of your hands. Don't pick up your pet by its tail. The tail skin is delicate and could tear if your grab it roughly.

A rat is agile, and you can easily teach it to stay on your shoulder. You should not have to worry about your pet falling off. Young rats learn how to "shoulder ride" better than do older rats, who seem to prefer the security of your hands.

Because your rat's nails are tiny and sharp, be sure to wear clothes that protect your shoulders. The first few times you put your rat on your shoulder, it might climb down and its toenails could scratch you. If your rat does climb down, put it back on your shoulder and keep your hand ready to steady it. Your rat can learn this quickly if you are patient and persistent.

Some pet rat owners carry their pet in a pocket or tucked in their sleeve. Rats like riding in sleeves. A rat will settle down comfortably, with its head poking out, sensing the world with its nose, ears, and eyes. Take care to protect your pet from falling out or from being bumped into another object if you carry it this way.

The more you handle your pet, the more quickly it will learn to trust you and become tame. A rat that is handled frequently makes a better pet than one that is left by itself for long periods of time. Scientific studies have shown that rats that are handled and played with are friendlier and even more intelligent than neglected rats. Play with your rat often, at least four or five times a week.

STARTING TAMING

You can start taming your rat by holding it in your hands and letting it get used to you. Stay near the cage and let your pet jump back into it when it wants. Curiosity will prompt it to climb back out of the cage to see you. You can also offer your pet a tasty treat. Taking your rat out consistently and playing with it will quickly tame your rat. By the end of the first week, your rat should know you and be tame, asking to come and play.

EXPLORING

Many pet owners allow their pet to explore and play in the room where they keep its cage. Let your rat begin its explorations from its cage, which it uses as a

Regularly playing with your rat will make it a friendlier and even more enjoyable pet.

familiar home base. Open the cage door and invite your rat to come out. (If your pet's home is an aquarium, you can use a ladder to let your pet climb in and out.) An exploring rat will poke its head out, dart back, look out again, and then venture forth.

You can assist your rat when it is first learning about the room in which its cage is kept. Your objective is to build your rat's confidence and avoid having it become frightened. While your rat is exploring, you can also begin training it to come to you when it is called. Sit or lie down a little distance from your rat's cage and don't make any sudden movements. Call your rat's name as it begins to leave its cage. Slowly move your hands toward your rat and call its name again. Because you and your hands should be as familiar to your rat as its cage is, it will scamper over to you. Pet it profusely and praise it.

Encourage your rat to return to its home base frequently by placing it back at its cage and letting it begin its exploration anew. By returning your rat to a familiar area (its cage), your pet won't become frightened and "lost" in an unknown area. A lost rat is one that has wandered too far into an unknown area and becomes frightened and hides. A scared rat might hide a long time before it feels it is safe to quickly run back to a familiar area. Your rat could become timid and less enjoyable for you if it is frightened too often.

You help build your rat's confidence by returning it to an area it knows. Some rats become very playful when you return them to their cage and will try to quickly bound past you to where they last left off exploring. This is a good sign because it indicates that your pet is confident and eager to explore. Your rat will develop a mental map of the area it is exploring. You will see your rat move quickly through places with which it is familiar and proceed more cautiously in unfamiliar areas.

Eventually, your rat will know the entire room and will then bound comfortably around the room. You will discover that your pet has favorite areas in which it likes to play. Be careful that your pet does not chew anything inappropriate when it is roaming. If you hear or see your rat do something you don't want it to do, try clapping your hands and shouting "no"! This will startle your pet so that it will stop. Of course, some rats are persistent, and it might be best to remove whatever they found so alluring. Rats are attracted to houseplants, and they should be out of your rat's reach when it is exploring. Not only will it dig in the soil, but it also might eat the plant. Because some houseplants are poisonous, you could end up with a sick rat. Be alert that your pet does not escape when it is exploring. (Note that most rats voluntarily return to their cage if they escape or get lost. Always place the cage on the floor, with food and water, and leave the door open.)

Once your pet knows its room well, you will find that it seeks you out to play. If your rat is walking around, call it to come to you. Because your pet likes to interact with you, it will come when called, especially if it is in a room with which it is already familiar.

You can play with your rat or give it a reward of food when it comes to you.

If you expose your rat to many new and different environments when it is young, it will not be as frightened of strange environments when it gets older. When your rat rides on your shoulder, it will experience new rooms, sights, smells, and sounds.

In any new location, you will notice that your pet repeats the same pattern as the one it used to explore the original room; it begins its explorations from something familiar (i.e., you) and returns to familiar areas before progressing farther. When it is frightened, your rat will come running back to you. When your rat starts to wander too far, encourage it to come back to you by calling its name. If you make a slight movement, it might frighten your rat and cause it to run back to you. Some people "train" their rat to climb up their leg when they are outside or in a strange room. They are actually using the rat's natural tendency to respond to the owner as a security base.

Some pet rats like to be toted around in their owner's pockets, which is why they are sometimes called "pocket pets." If you are going to carry your rat in this manner, use caution to prevent it from falling out.

RAT BEHAVIORS

Your pet displays a variety of behaviors in response to different stimuli. Recognizing and understanding your rat's body language and behavior will help you to tame and train it.

A nervous or frightened rat might rapidly groom itself, or freeze in one spot, lying low against the ground with a blank look on its face. If you are holding your pet, you might feel it shiver repeatedly. Another sign of fear is body elimination in the form of a dropping. This is part of the body's "fight or flight" mechanism. A nervous or frightened rat will not eat. If you are trying to train your rat by using food, it must be calm and relaxed in order to eat the reward.

animal's body. They help tell the rat more about its environment.

Out in the open, especially in new territory, rats proceed cautiously: scampering forward, crouching and pausing before moving, or running quickly to the nearest object to hide under or behind if frightened. This behavior

"Shoulder riding." This is another favorite activity for some pet rats. The first few times that you attempt this, be sure to wear protective clothing so that your pet's nails won't scratch you. Also, you should have your hand ready to steady your pet so that it doesn't run down your arm.

You might notice that when your pet is exploring in a room, it likes to run next to the walls. Rats prefer to run along walls or between objects with which they can keep their whiskers and guard hairs in contact. Their guard hairs are highly sensitive vibrissae, which are scattered throughout their fur. These hairs are more sensitive than the shorter hairs covering the

protects rats in the wild from being an obvious target for predators. Your pet rat will eventually bound comfortably in the room if no loud noises or sudden movements frighten it. If frightened, your rat will seek a hiding place.

You can tell your rat is contented if it grinds its teeth together. If you hold its head in your hand with your fingers under the chin and the palm of your hand over its head, your pet might start to grind its teeth. Some rats not only grind their teeth but might also lick your hand.

PLAYING

You can learn to play-fight with your pet by pretending your hand is another rat. Using one hand, gently grab your rat around the head or shoulders with your thumb on one side of its body and your first two fingers on the other side. Gently shake your fingers, moving your rat back and forth. Then pull your hand away, pause, and spring it forward and repeat the step again. Or you can *lightly* pinch your rat in repetitive moves, darting your hand back and forth to encourage it to get frisky. Alternatively, you can bounce your fingers up and down in front of your rat.

Most rats will respond by springing playfully forward and tackling your hand. When your rat tackles your fingers, you can wiggle them in protest or keep them still to let it know you are defeated and it has won. Your rat also might flip over onto its back,

and you can then tickle its belly. Some rats get very excited and carried away with this game and will scrabble all over your fingers, tackling and nibbling them. If your pet should happen to accidentally hurt you (this is rare), squeak loudly and play dead with your hand, or use your other hand to push it away (gently). If it rebounds with even more gusto, you can hold your hand firmly down on it or carry it away from you to a distant part of the room.

You can play keep-away with your rat. You will need a piece of yarn or tissue paper. Drag the yarn around in circles, and your rat will try to pounce on it and carry it off, much like a kitten plays with a ball of string. If you drag tissue paper around, your rat will leap after it, trying to catch it. Try balling up the paper and tossing it a short distance. Your pet might run after it, pick it up, and try to take it away. You can also play keep-away with a nut. Tie a string around a large nut (e.g., Brazil nuts work well) and move the nut around for your pet to chase. Your rat will be more likely to respond if you jerk the yarn, tissue paper, or nut (with lots of starts and stops.)

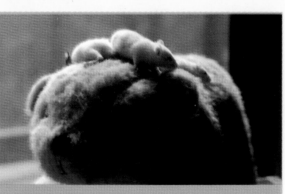

These rats enjoy playing atop a stuffed toy. If you are going to give your rat free access to certain areas of your home, supervision is a must.

A black hooded rat working out. Pet shops carry a wide variety of toys designed for rats and other small mammals.

TRAINING

Rats are used in behavioral studies by scientists and by students of all ages, from grade schools to colleges. They are particularly useful in experiments involving intelligence because they have higher IQs than mice and most other laboratory animals. Rats also learn to solve problems faster than the other small laboratory animals. From these experiments, scientists gain valuable insight into the basic steps of learning. Of course, they must draw their conclusions carefully, because rats are not nearly as intelligent and complex as humans.

Students at one college in the US train their rats to do complicated tricks and then hold a Rat Olympics, where their rats compete against each other. The students, in their psychology classes, apply the concepts of learning to a fun and educational activity. You don't need to be a college student to train your rat to learn these same complicated feats, such as playing soccer or hurdle racing. This section will help you learn the proper techniques to train your rat. With patience, persistence, and flexibility, you, too, can train your rat to perform complex tricks. Even if your rat is just a pet, it is still challenging and rewarding to try to train it.

Training your rat is different from taming and playing with it. Before you train your rat, you should always have a specific goal in mind (e.g., training your rat to walk a short distance on its hind legs). You should also be certain that your rat can actually do what you are asking of it. If your plan does not seem to be working, change it.

A good trainer uses an individual rat's natural talents to train the rat to do seemingly complicated feats. You, too, should find out what your rat enjoys doing. Some rats are good at jumping, while others are better at climbing. (It is the same as if you are talented at running but not catching.) Ideally, you have been playing with your rat and know what it likes to do. By incorporating its natural tendencies into tricks, you will reinforce what the rat already enjoys.

METHOD OF APPROXIMATION

The type of training you will use is called the method of approximation, or shaping. You will shape your rat's behavior by rewarding those behaviors that are close to the behavior you want; and as you train it, you will have your rat do a little more until it is eventually doing exactly what you want. You will use a reward of food to change and reinforce your rat's behavior.

Most rats learn best if the reward is some kind of food they find especially tasty, for example, sweetened cereals, cookies, and soft candy. As stated in the feeding chapter, these foods are not the best kind to feed your rat (they don't promote longevity).

But, they are usually what works best for training. Other kinds of food, such as oats and dog food, are too mundane and your pet won't be willing to work to get them. However, it is always worth a try to get your rat to respond to some kind of healthier food as a reward. Pet stores stock healthy treats that your pet might find appealing.

reward with its assignment for no longer than 25 seconds. If you wait too long to reward your rat, it will not make the connection between the food reward and its action.

Constant reinforcement with food is needed only for the learning stages of a trick. Once your rat learns a given behavior, you will switch to a variable

Food rewards are necessary in the early stages of training for a particular desired behavior.

Always give a small, "rat-sized" piece of food! If you give your rat too large a piece, it will quickly fill up and will no longer respond to your training attempts. Give your rat the food reward immediately after it has done what you wanted it to do. A rat associates the food

schedule of reinforcement. Reinforcing a learned behavior only occasionally is more effective for maintaining the behavior than a constant predictable schedule of reinforcement. When you reinforce the learned behavior at random, your rat will work harder to try and get a reward of food. Once you are able to reinforce a learned behavior only occasionally, you can use your food reward to reinforce the best examples of the behavior. Other kinds of positive reinforcement (besides food) that you can give your rat include petting and enthusiastic praise.

Your rat might not respond to a food reward for a number of reasons. If your rat stops eating the food reward, it might be that it is tired of the food; and you need to try a new kind. Every rat has its personal preference. Again, be certain that you are not giving your rat too large a piece. If your rat won't eat the food at all, it could be that it is too nervous to eat. You should handle your pet more, to make it tamer and feel secure.

If your rat does not have enough of a sweet tooth to be tempted by the reward, you might need to restrict the amount of food in its regular diet. This option should not be approached lightly. It means that you must monitor your rat's weight extremely carefully. You do not want your rat to lose more than five percent of its original body weight, unless you are training an older rat that is overweight. This means that if your rat weighs 275 grams (10oz.), it cannot lose more than 14 grams ($^{1}/_{2}$oz.). If you are using a young rat, it can't lose even five percent of its weight because it is still growing.

To weigh your rat, you will need access to a balance-beam scale or a scale that can measure weight in grams. Before you start food restriction, weigh your rat to get its initial weight. Keep your rat on the food restriction diet until it begins to respond to the food rewards, and then give it just enough food so that it can maintain its weight. Weigh your rat at the same time each day. Feed your rat its regular diet (the restricted amount) after the end of each day's training period. If it looks as though your rat is getting thin, take it off the restricted diet and let it feed freely until its weight is at the pre-training level.

Training should be enjoyable for you and your pet. Give your pet the opportunity to play for a little while before beginning a training session.

THE TRAINING PROCESS

When training your rat to perform a single act, such as jumping or climbing up or across something, you start by rewarding your rat for exhibiting the behavior for a short distance or time. (It is sometimes possible to teach your rat a single behavior without the use of food as a reward, but your rat will not perform as consistently.)

Walking on Hind Legs. Suppose that you want to teach your rat to stand and walk a short distance on its hind legs. You start by rewarding your rat when it merely stands up on its hind legs. Hold the food reward where your rat can see or smell it when it is on all fours, and then move the reward above its head so that the rat stands up to get it. You can also say "up" to your rat at the same time. Eventually, you will require your rat to stay on its hind legs for longer periods before you reward it. Continue this method by moving the reward a little in front of your standing rat, so that it has to walk to reach the reward. You can gradually extend the distance it has to walk on its hind legs until it has reached your preset goal.

Walking a Tightrope. The same method can be used to train your rat to walk a tightrope (e.g., a $1/4$ in. wooden dowel or a climbing rope that is at least 1 in. thick.) The rope should be no more than a few feet off the ground. Tying or supporting it between two chairs works well. Of

Rats are very agile, and with proper training they can be taught to jump from one spot to another.

course, you should have pillows (or some similar objects) to cushion your rat should it fall. However, you should not have to worry about your rat falling as long as you don't use a narrower rope.

Suppose that you are using a rope that is 3 ft. long. You will start by putting your rat about 6 in. from the *finish*. Then reward your rat when it crosses the 6 in.

The reward should always be located or given to the rat from the same place. Slowly increase the distance the rat must cross to obtain the reward. That is, move your rat 9 in. from the end, then 12 in., and so forth. You might wonder why your rat begins at the finish of the rope instead of at the beginning. This is because your rat moves more quickly toward areas it already knows (i.e., your rat moves from an area it is not sure of into a reinforced, familiar area.)

More Than One Trick. To train for a series of behaviors, you must also begin at the *end* and work backwards as your rat becomes adept in performing each desired action. Suppose that you have built a complex obstacle course that requires your rat to go through a tunnel, climb a rope, jump from one platform to another, climb up a ladder and walk down a ramp, go through the black door (not the white door), and then push a ball into a cup. You will start by training your rat to push the ball into the cup.

The hardest part of the obstacle course is teaching your rat to put the ball into the cup, because this is an unnatural activity for a rat. Start by rewarding your rat for putting its nose near the ball, with further rewards as your rat touches the ball with its nose, then pushes the ball in the direction of the cup, and so forth.

To help with this unnatural activity and any other group of activities, you will probably have to use a secondary reinforcer. A secondary reinforcer is a signal that tells your rat that a food reward is available. Noises usually work best, for example, a loud click or a short whistle. Always use the same secondary reinforcer.

To train your rat to recognize the secondary reinforcer, start with a food reward in a small container, such as a jar lid. For example, if you want your rat to put a ball in a cup, you might put the food reward in the jar lid directly into the cup. When your rat discovers the reward, make the sound of your secondary reinforcer, and repeat it a few times. Gradually increase the distance that your rat has to cover to get the food reward. Sound the reinforcer when your rat is farther away from the food lid. Your rat should hurry to get the reward. If it does not, it is possible that the distance between the reward and rat is too far. Repeat the secondary reinforcer until your rat has learned where the reward is and goes to it when you sound the secondary reinforcer. When your rat has made the connection between the secondary reinforcer and the reward, you can train it for more complicated behaviors.

After you have trained your rat to put the ball in the cup, move your rat farther back along the obstacle course, a little at a time (no more than a few inches every three or four runs). Your rat will learn some things, such as going down the ramp, very quickly. Other activities will be learned more slowly. If your rat suddenly stops improving, it might be that you are asking it to make too large a step from one trick to the next. You should break the steps down into small increments so that it is easy for your rat to constantly improve. Even if this is only inch by inch, your rat will reach your goal much faster than if you try to force rapid progress in large steps. Also, it might be that you need to rethink your shaping procedure and try another tack.

You do not want to tire your rat or discourage it. Stay alert to signs that your rat is not enjoying the training. Training sessions should last between 20 to 45 minutes a day. You can have one training session or two short training sessions, one in the morning, and another in the afternoon. However, this will depend on your rat's attention span, the difficulty of the trick, and the enjoyment it gets from training. Your rat will have "off" days just like you. You should always end the training session with a positive experience (i.e., quit while you are ahead). The last behavior of the training session should be a good reinforceable performance. It is exciting to see your pet perform three or four good responses in a row. But resist the temptation to see or do it again. Your rat might soon tire and mistakes will appear, and the training session will end poorly.

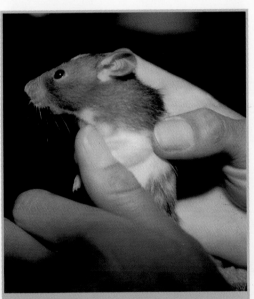

A rat that has been properly socialized will not resist being held. In fact, it may enjoy it.

Building an Obstacle Course. Building your own obstacle course is challenging and fun. If you are clever, you can build one that has moveable and interchangeable parts. In other words, you can attach each component to different areas of the course. If you can rearrange the obstacle course, it will continue to be challenging and fun for your rat. Items such as ladders, balls, seesaws, bells, mirrors, ramps, ropes, doors, and so forth can be included in your obstacle course. The base of the obstacle course can be made of $1/4$ in. plywood or some other strong material, such as particle board. The obstacle course does not have to be covered with screening. You can create a horizontal obstacle course, or you can design it so that it is vertical.

first, your rat will make mistakes, but each time it goes through, it will remember more of its past mistakes and make the trip more rapidly. Eventually your rat will go through the maze without making any mistakes at all. You can time your rat's runs through the maze and make a graph of how quickly it improves (e.g., the

It's amazing what rats can do. These hobbyists are training a rat to run hurdles.

Building a Maze. You can also construct a maze for your rat. A maze is a confusing network of passages, most of which lead to dead ends. There is usually only one way to get to the reward of food at the end of the maze. Your rat will learn how to negotiate the maze through trial and error. At

number of attempts would be on the horizontal axis and the time taken would be on the vertical axis). You can also compare how quickly different rats learn the same maze.

It is a lot of fun to construct and design a maze. As with the obstacle course, try to make it so that the position of the walls can be changed. You can make a maze from cardboard, masking tape, and string. A more permanent maze can be constructed of $^1/_4$ in. plywood. You might want to cover the maze with wire screening or provide extra height on the sides so that your rat cannot just hop out. However, some people leave

your rat could develop bad habits, which might make it more difficult to train to that course.

Other Activities. Using the same techniques just described, you can train your rat to (1) select one letter of the alphabet from a row of mixed letters; (2) identify an advertisement or a product from a dozen assorted ads; (3)

A soccer match in progress. When training your pet, don't overtire it: a training session should last no longer than about 45 minutes a day.

the maze uncovered to show that their rats stay in the maze because they like it. Indeed, most rats are happiest when they are busy exploring and learning. However, it is best not to let your pet play unsupervised on any course that you want to train it to use (e.g., time its runs), because

learn to distinguish a specific design on a door that has food behind it from doors that do not (e.g., you can use different patterns of bold stripes, or you can use symbols such as diamonds or circles); and (4) learn to identify a door with food behind it based on three different colors

Walking a high wire is one of the more challenging training activities for rats.

(e.g., black, gray, and white). You can also combine any of these activities into an obstacle course.

Rats can even be trained to play a version of rat soccer or basketball. You should have two teams, consisting of one rat each. The rats should be the same sex (females are less likely to fight than males, but they can get ornery when they are in heat). You can find small rat-sized soccer balls or basketballs at a toy store. Again, using the same methods of shaping and a secondary reinforcer, you can train your rat to pick up the ball and place it in the right net. Always place the food reward (in a jar lid) in the same location. The net is probably the best location because that is where your rat will be bringing the ball, and it can get its reward right there.

You can also train your rat to run hurdles and compete against another rat. The hurdle course can be built using a piece of plywood that is 5 ft. long. Put two runs on the same board but separate them with a piece of wood that is high enough to prevent a rat from easily jumping to the other side. Space the wooden hurdles every 6 to 12 in. Train your rat to rapidly run to the end of the finish line, where it will be rewarded. Once your rat knows this, you can race two rats together.

Use your imagination and creativity to train your rat to do seemingly elaborate acts. For example, one college student trained a rat to climb up a ramp disguised as a snow-covered mountain, pick up a small doll that was buried in the snow, take it down the mountain on a stretcher, and bring it to a first-aid tent. Another student trained a rat to be Tarzan. The rat climbed a wooden ladder up a rat-sized tree; crossed a suspension bridge; went down a ramp into a swamp where it picked up "Jane" (a small doll) from the mouth of a plastic alligator; and then took Jane to safety.

Rats learn differently at different ages. You can test your rat in any of these situations and see if it improves as it gets older, or if its rate of learning decreases once it is a comparatively old rat.

Finally, training your rat should be a fun and rewarding experience for both you and your rat. While it takes work and time, the results are well worth it. Remember to remain sensitive to the nuances of your rat's moods. For example, let your rat play for a short while before beginning a training session. Train only one behavior at a time and don't interrupt the training session without reason. Also, if more than one person will be training the rat, each of them should train a separate trick to avoid confusing the rat. You will be amazed at how smart your rat is and the clever things you can train it to do. Use your imagination and creativity to think of new tricks to teach your pet.

A pregnant agouti rex rat. The gestation period in rats is between 21 and 23 days.

BREEDING

Breeding rats is an interesting and fun experience. It is a joy to watch the young rats grow from small pink creatures into furry bouncy rats. However, there are some important points you should consider before you breed your rat. A mother rat requires a big cage, at least 24 in. long by 12 in. wide by 12 in. high. She will need plenty of room to organize her nest, food area, and toilet. She also needs space where she can retreat from the babies when they become too demanding. The baby rats will need lots of room in which to run and play. It will take you more time to care for a mother rat with babies. For instance, you will need to clean the cage more often.

Before breeding your pet, you should make sure that you can find homes for the young rats.

BREEDING SYSTEMS

Commercial breeders who need to produce large numbers of rats usually use the polygamous or harem system of breeding. One male is typically housed with from two to six females. Naturally, a large cage is used. The pregnant females are moved to separate cages before giving birth. By removing the females, it has been found that they produce more milk and larger babies and litters. The females are returned to the harem after their young are weaned. Some breeders move the male from cage to cage. Each cage has a single female. The male remains for one week in each cage. He is always removed before the birth of the young. The male is reintroduced just after a female's babies are weaned. One male is used for every seven females.

The monogamous system of breeding involves the pairing of one male and one female. The pair are kept together even when the female has babies. Most pet rat owners who want to breed their female "just once" use this system.

If you decide that you would like to breed pet rats on a large scale, you should use the harem system of breeding. Select only healthy rats with good temperament and no physical deformities. Ideally, you should use rats that produce large litters. You also need to consider the fertility of both the female and male.

BREEDING AND PREGNANCY

Rats can produce young when they are only 50 to 60 days old. However, the best age at which to begin breeding pet rats is when they are three to four months old. Breeding a female rat too early might stunt her growth and result in small, weak offspring. Females should weigh at least 250 grams (8 $^3/_4$ oz.) and males at least 300 grams (10 $^1/_2$ oz.).

A female rat's estrus cycle lasts four to five days. The estrus period when she can get pregnant lasts 12 hours and usually begins in late afternoon or evening. If

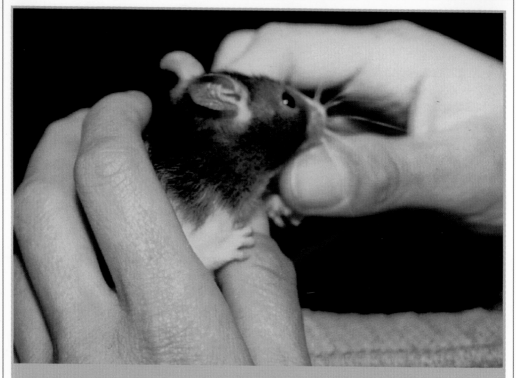

Male rats are referred to as bucks; female rats are called does.

you keep your pet female rat with a male rat for at least a week, she should get pregnant.

Within 48 hours of giving birth, the female also has a fertile estrus period, called the postpartum estrus. This means that if she is kept with a male during this time, she will most likely become pregnant again. If you want only one litter of baby rats, remove the male before the babies are born.

The gestation period (the amount of time it takes the young to develop in the mother) is between 21 and 23 days. However, the gestation period can be longer if the mating takes place almost immediately after the female gives birth (the postpartum estrus): when

pregnancy and the nursing of young occur simultaneously, implantation of fertile eggs can be delayed for three to seven days and therefore lengthen the gestation period. About two weeks after mating, you should be able to tell if the female is pregnant by the firm swelling of her lower abdomen.

A female rat may have a reproductive breeding life of 9 to 16 months. During this time, she can bear 7 to 10 litters with 6 to 14 offspring per litter. An average litter size is 8; larger litters of up to 20 pups are rare. (The male and female are variously referred to as the sire and dam, or the buck and doe. Baby rats are called pups, kittens, or neonates.) A female rat older than one year will eventually have a decrease in litter size and an increase in the length of time between litters. A female's ability to reproduce ends at 15 to 18 months.

A pregnant female rat has a large appetite. The energy requirements of a female rat during gestation are up to one third more than when she is not pregnant. Be sure to always have plenty of high-quality food available for the female (i.e., free-feed).

The female's nest-building activities will increase in the last days of her pregnancy. Provide her with an ample supply of nest material such as clean unprinted paper, tissue paper (unscented), or an old soft shirt. She will build her nest by piling shavings into a corner and shredding the nesting material that you have given her. (Pure cedar shavings are not recommended as they have been linked to instances of litter desertion.)

THE BIRTH

The birth itself usually lasts about one and a half hours but can take anywhere from half an hour up to almost four hours. The larger the litter, the more time it will take. The litter size can depend upon the fecundity of the strain, how well-fed the female was, and her age, among other factors.

A well-handled female rat that knows you usually does not mind if you quickly look at the babies. However, you must be careful

This agouti rex was a winner in the AOC (Any Other Color) class.

A young Siamese female rat. A female rat may have a reproductive breeding life of 9 to 16 months.

because she might become defensive and bite you. Any other rats in the cage with the mother will also defend and protect the pups. If you are curious and want to see the babies, it is best to distract the female's attention, or have someone hold her while you look. After peeking once, leave the babies alone until they leave the nest.

The mother rat instinctively knows how to care for her young. She licks the babies all over, including their tiny rear ends. This stimulates their digestive system. If the mother drags any of the babies out of the nest, she will pick them up and return them to the nest. She will also retrieve any babies that crawl out of the nest.

The female rat's food requirement increases dramatically when she is nursing her young (called lactation). She can eat her own weight in food in just two days. Feed her two to three times what you normally would and make sure she has food available.

Because she is eating more, there will be more droppings in the cage, and you must remove them. Sometimes the female removes the dirty portions of the nest, which you can then discard. When cleaning the cage, it is best to leave the nest alone until the babies are two weeks old. You can then clean the nest by partially removing any dirty material and leaving the remainder intact. Give the

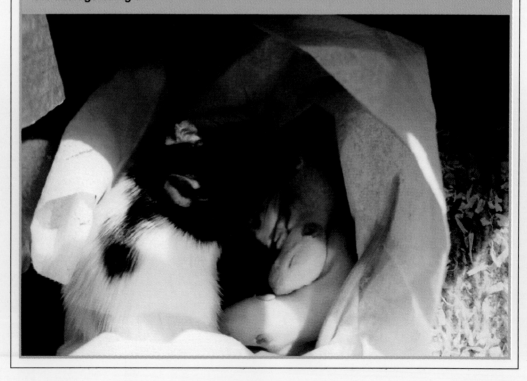

A mother rat keeping watch over her litter. A rat litter can range from 6 to 16 in size, with the average being 8.

A two-week-old litter. Note that body markings are already evident.

mother replacement nesting material.

THE YOUNG RATS

Young rats are born hairless, and their eyes and ear canals are covered with skin. The babies weigh about $^1/_6$ oz. (5 to 6 grams) at birth. In two to four days, their ears open. You might hear the babies make peeping noises when the mother enters or leaves the nest. When alarmed, baby rats can call their mother with ultrasonic cries. The mother's ears and whiskers might twitch when she hears these high-pitched sounds.

By the time the pups are one week old, a soft coat of fuzz is discernible. You can usually even tell approximately what colors the babies will be. Their first teeth appear at the age of eight to ten days. The babies' eyes open when they are about 14 to 15 days old. The young rats grow rapidly. At two and a half weeks, they will start to explore the nest and follow their mother. At this age, they have large heads with squinty eyes, bright coats, and look like little puppy dogs. They will start to eat solid food and play-fight with each other.

Make sure the water bottle is low enough for them to reach. They will learn to drink from it by watching their mother. Always have food available for the mother and babies. You will be surprised at how much they can eat. A young rat's balance is unsteady, and it will teeter when it picks up its first piece of food to hold in its hands. However, its sense of balance will get better. With more rats eating, you will find that you need to clean the cage more often.

Young rats are very active; they bounce all over the cage and are great fun to watch and to play with. You can play with the babies by letting them smell your hands when you feed them and clean their cage. A baby rat may run back to its nest, but it will soon return to investigate your hands. The young rats will quickly become used to you and make better pets because of their contact with you.

By three weeks of age, the young rats can weigh 1.8 ounces (50 grams). They can be weaned (leave their mother) between three to four weeks of age. Some rats seem to grow bigger if they are not weaned until the fourth week. At six weeks, they should be kept in single-sex groups. They will reach sexual maturity by two months of age.

LITTER DESERTION

Abandoned pups are not common. Some of the factors that might cause a mother rat to desert her young include a lack of privacy, excessive noise, overcrowding, a dirty cage, lack of nesting material, or injured young. Note that you can prevent most of these factors. You can attempt to get another currently nursing female to foster nurse the deserted young by rubbing a little mentholated petroleum jelly on both batches of young and on the nursing female's nose.

If you don't have another female, you can attempt to raise the babies yourself by using a commercial puppy-or kitten-milk formula available at pet shops. You can feed the formula from a nursing bottle, which many pet shops carry specifically for orphaned animals. Give frequent small feedings; you will have to use your own judgment to see that the babies are not overfed. You should also stimulate their digestive system by wiping their rear ends with a damp warm cloth after feeding. You can keep the pups warm if you put a blanket wrapped around a heating pad into the cage. Or, you can set up an incandescent light, being careful that it is high enough to prevent the pups from being burned. At about two weeks of age, start to provide the babies with bread soaked in the formula.

SELECTIVE BREEDING

Selective breeding is the process people use to breed only those animals with certain characteristics. For example, the great variety of dog breeds found today were produced through selective breeding. Breeders use only those animals with the desired color, conformation (shape), temperament, and behavior (e.g., retrieving). To properly practice selective breeding, you also need to have an understanding of the principles of genetics, which is the science of heredity. This is because there is an important distinction between the physical appearance of an animal (the phenotype) and its genetic make-up (the genotype). Two individuals can have the same physical appearance but different gene combinations, and their offspring will be correspondingly different. Understandable discussions on genetics can be found in other books available in pet shops and libraries and are worth reading if you intend to selectively breed your rats.

Fancy rat strains, such as the Himalayans and rexes, have all been developed through selective breeding. You might find that there is greater demand for some of these strains (such as the Himalayans) because they are still relatively uncommon. (If you cannot find these types of rats in your area, contact a fancy rat club).

If you do decide to selectively breed rats, it is important that you keep written records. Although you might view this as a form of work, such records will allow you to recognize and trace the offspring of a particular mating. By studying your records, you will be able to tell which rats are most prolific and how the color combinations are passed on.

Rats can be weaned between three to four weeks of age. They experience a rapid rate of development, so a litter should be separated into single-sex groups at six weeks of age to prevent unwanted breedings.

RAT SHOWS

Pet rat shows are held in some parts of the country. Rats are judged on the basis of their conformation, color, type, and temperament. If you want to show rats, you will need to have animals that conform as closely as possible to the official show standard. Show-quality rats are usually produced through careful breeding. If there are no rat shows in your area, you should get a copy of a rules and standards book. You can then try to set up your own rat shows. Besides rat shows, you can also hold contests to competitively demonstrate the intelligence of your rat (similar to field trials for dogs, in which the dogs perform a routine and compete against each other).

HEALTH

Prevention is the best method for keeping your pet healthy. There are some simple steps you can take to help your pet stay well. First, start with a healthy rat. This means that no matter how attractively colored a particular rat might be, if you hear it wheezing, don't bring it home. Second, keep cages and accessories clean. Don't let the cage become dirty and a breeding ground for disease-causing bacteria. Third, feed a variety of fresh foods so your pet gets all the nutrients it needs. While your pet will eat almost anything and show a special fondness for treats such as cookies, resist feeding it these treats too often. Fourth, always have clean, fresh water available for your rat. Finally, attentive observation of your pet will help you detect any changes in its appearance or appetite that could signal an illness.

Some rats can be infected with a disease-causing organism but not show any signs of the disease. (This condition is called asymptomatic or subclinical.) Stressful conditions such as shipping, overcrowding, drafts, or sudden temperature changes might cause the disease to become active. Disease-causing organisms are spread in a number of ways. They can be transmitted in the air; through contaminated shavings, food, water bottles, and even your hands; or by a mother to her young. Rats are hardy creatures but can develop illnesses in an environment of neglect.

Most of the illnesses your pet rat can contract mean an immediate trip to the veterinarian, especially those listed under "Infectious Diseases." Your veterinarian will prescribe a medicine or other course of action. Be sure to follow directions with any medicines you are given. If your veterinarian gives you an antibiotic to dissolve in your pet's water, ask if you should use distilled water (to prevent scaling of the water bottle and inadequate uptake of the antibiotic). You should also ask if you should add sugar to the solution to make it taste better (and if so, how much). Store medicines out of your rat's reach and dispose of them after the expiration date.

Your veterinarian will usually treat your rat symptomatically. This means that the veterinarian will treat the signs of the disease, without confirming the exact cause of the disease. For example, if your rat wheezes when it breathes, the veterinarian will most likely give an antibiotic to control the respiratory distress. The veterinarian will not necessarily diagnose the exact disease-causing organism, because to do so requires a culture (the organism is grown in a Petri dish so that it can be identified), which might be time-consuming, expensive, and not easily available. Many diseases can be identified only after the animal has died.

If your rat does get sick, there are some steps you can take to hasten its recovery and prevent the disease from spreading to any other rats you might have. A sick rat should be immediately isolated. You can place the sick rat in a carrying cage. These cages are small, partially enclosed, and easier to keep warm than wire cages. If you keep your rat in its regular cage, remove any obstacles that might bother it (e.g., ladders, bells). Make sure your rat has easy access to both food and water unless your veterinarian directs you otherwise. Change the food and water daily and keep the bedding clean and dry. Give your pet an additional cloth to stay warm. The cage in which a sick rat was kept should be sterilized. A disinfectant such as bleach can be used.

The following is a description of the diseases that your pet rat can contract.

INFECTIOUS DISEASES

Labyrinthitis. A bacterial infection of your rat's inner ear will cause tilting of the head (called torticollis). Your rat might move in circles and have difficulty getting up. This infection is often associated with upper respiratory infections. It can be treated with antibiotics.

Red Eye. Behind the rat's eye lies a pigmented gland called the harderian gland. This gland secretes a red-brown material (porphyrins) mixed with tears that lubricates the eye and eyelid. Infections, irritation, and inflammation from within the eye can all cause red excretions or a red circle around the eye. You should be alert to the presence of "red tears" as an indication that your pet might be sick and need treatment from a veterinarian.

Murine Respiratory Mycoplasmosis. The most common ailment seen in pet rats is murine respiratory mycoplasmosis (referred to as MRM). Rats (and mice) are the principle hosts of the disease-causing bacterium, *Mycoplasma pulmonis.* This infection might be subclinical, with signs of infection difficult to detect. The clinical onset is usually slow and progressive, but acute episodes can occur in young and susceptible animals.

This disease is highly contagious. It is not possible to cure an infected animal. The disease is transmitted in a number of ways, including direct contact between mother and young, and even when the young are still developing in the mother (*in utero* transmission). Some rats exposed to the disease never display any symptoms. However, stress or other bacterial infections can cause a rat to suddenly exhibit symptoms. Most pet rats can live normally when this disease affects the upper respiratory tract, but when it becomes more severe (bronchopulmonary syndrome), the rat can die after several weeks or months.

The symptoms of upper respiratory disease include sneezing, sniffling, and rough hair. If the inner ear becomes involved, head tilt can occur. This disease can become aggravated by other bacterial infections, Sendai virus infection, or ammonia (from urine). It is then called bronchopulmonary syndrome. Signs of infection with bronchopulmonary syndrome include lethargy, rough hair, hunched posture, chattering, weight loss, labored breathing, and eventual death. The bacteria can also infect the genital tract and cause infertility, resorption of embryos, and small litters.

If your pet is infected with MRM, you can take some precautions to prevent the development of the disease into bronchopulmonary syndrome. A clean cage is essential because the presence of ammonia can aggravate your rat's condition. A dirty cage is also an invitation for other infections. Avoid stressing your pet (e.g., don't bring it outside where it could get chilled). In most cases, your pet rat can still live a long life with occasional severe bouts. An antibiotic such as tetracycline hydrochloride can be obtained from your veterinarian. Prescribed at 5 mg/ml fresh sweetened water, changed daily for five days, it often suppresses clinical signs. It is recommended that you use the antibiotic therapy only for severe bouts that your pet might have, as a means of making it more comfortable.

Scientists have been able to eliminate this disease in experimental rat colonies by treating pregnant females with oxytetracycline, hysterectomy, and foster nursing on *Mycoplasma*-free mothers. There is ongoing experimental development of vaccines for this illness.

Other Bacteria-caused Illnesses. Illnesses caused by other disease organisms can also show symptoms similar to those of MRM. There are some ways that you can distinguish among them. Murine respiratory mycoplasmosis usually does not cause a precipitous decline in your rat's health. In other words, MRM is chronic, and your pet can live many years with no change in condition. The other illnesses will cause a more abrupt change in your pet and are more likely to cause death.

Symptoms associated with the more serious organisms (including *Salmonella, Streptococcus pneumoniae, S. zooepidemicus, Pasteurella pneumotropica,* and *Corynebacterium kutscheri*) include the sudden onset of sneezing, nasal and eye discharge, loss of appetite, weight loss, labored breathing, hunched posture, listlessness, abscesses, and abnormal gait. An animal with Salmonellosis can also have diarrhea. Torticollis (head tilt) can be seen in animals infected with *S. pneumoniae.* Abscesses (visible to you on or underneath the skin) are associated with *P. pneumotropica,* whereas abnormal gait is most often associated with *C. kutscheri.*

These bacterial diseases are treated with antibiotics, but in most cases treatment is difficult because the condition is usually advanced at the time of detection. For example, benzathine penicillin (150 units/gram body weight) has been recommended for rats infected with *Streptococcus,* and chloramphenicol and ampicillin have been used to treat animals infected with *P. pneumontropica.*

rats that are older than eighteen months. These tumors can be surgically removed but usually recur. It is important to have them removed early because large tumors are more difficult to remove. In some cases, a relationship between tumor development and obesity has been found. Slim rats are less prone to

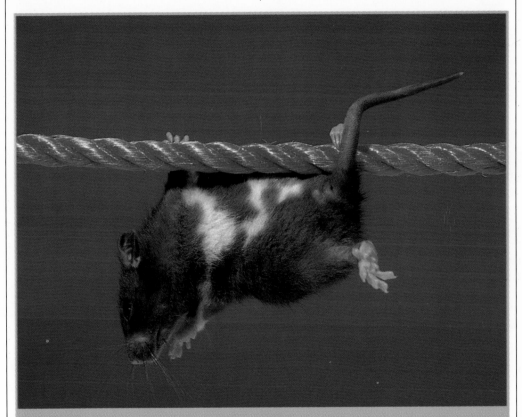

A young chocolate female rat. A healthy rat is alert and active. If there is a marked change in your pet's behavior, you should consult a veterinarian who specializes in small animals.

Your veterinarian will advise you on the most appropriate course of treatment.

NONINFECTIOUS DISEASES
Tumors. Benign mammary tumors might appear in female

tumors. A high-fiber, low-fat diet has reduced the incidence of these tumors.
Slobbering. Threads of saliva that appear around the rat's mouth are referred to as slobbers. They can be caused by a

A rat with a large, but benign, tumor. Such tumors can be surgically removed, but in many cases they will grow back.

malocclusion of the front incisor teeth. Malocclusion means that the teeth do not meet properly, and your pet might be unable to eat. Malocclusion of the teeth can be genetic, dietary, or due to infections. You will need to take your pet to a veterinarian, who will trim your rat's teeth.

Ringtail. Ringtail results in the loss of part or all of the tail. The tail will have constrictions with some swelling. The rat will otherwise appear healthy. This disease usually occurs during the cold season when the humidity is low (less than 20%) in artificially heated rooms. It might be that this dry air causes an abnormal response of the temperature-regulating vessels in the tails of young rats. Wire cages and

excessive ventilation can predispose rats to the disease. Ringtail can be prevented by providing solid-bottom plastic cages with adequate bedding and raising the humidity in the room to approximately 50% (e.g., place a bowl of water near a heater outlet).

Chronic Renal Disease. This disease is usually found in certain strains of rats, such as the Sprague-Dawley and Wistar. Both are albino strains. Symptoms of the disease include excessive or increased water consumption and increased urination. If your rat is affected, you might notice that it drinks its bottle of water much faster than usual and that the cage smells more strongly of urine. Diabetes can cause these same symptoms, so it is necessary for your veterinarian to perform a diagnostic test. A rat with chronic renal disease is put on a low-protein, low-salt diet.

Internal Parasites. Pinworms inhabit the intestinal tract of a rat and can result in diminished weight gain, diarrhea, and a decrease in activity. Tapeworms can also cause similar symptoms, including pot belly. A veterinarian can determine whether your pet rat is infected by examining fresh droppings under a microscope. If your pet has internal parasites, the veterinarian will prescribe the appropriate medicine for that parasite.

External Parasites. Parasites such as fleas and lice are rarely found on pet rats. Fleas can be transferred from other animals in the family, such as a dog or cat. Excessive scratching or the presence of fleas on your pet indicates an infestation. Use a cat flea-and-tick powder or spray to eliminate the fleas on your rat. Observe the following precautions when using a powder or spray: 1.) If you use a powder, take care that neither you nor the rat inhale any of the dust. 2.) Hold the canister low and cover your rat's face. 3.) If you use a spray, either cover the rat's face with your hand to protect its eyes, or spray some on a cloth and then apply it to the affected area.

Because the life cycle of the flea takes place on the host animal and its living quarters, it is important to also treat your pet's cage. Lice can be treated with a spray formulated for birds. If you have difficulties eliminating these pests, consult a veterinarian.

The abscess on this rex rat is slowly starting to heal after it was opened and drained.

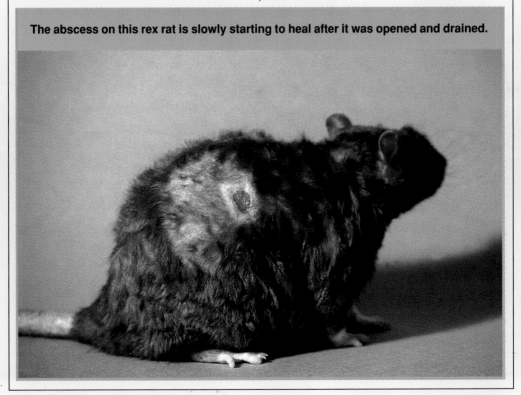

Ulcerative Dermatitis. The symptoms of ulcerative dermatitis are scabs, bald spots, and excessive scratching around the neck, head, and tail base. The bacterium *Staphylococcus aureus* is often associated with the wounds. Some rats that scratch excessively can be considered to have a vice. A topical antibiotic ointment with cortisone (to help stop the itchiness the rat feels) can be prescribed by your veterinarian to apply to the wounds. Your rat might lick the medicine. If so, try applying it and then take your rat out to play so it is less inclined to lick the medicine.

It might also help to trim the toenails on your rat's hind feet. Use clippers designed for birds or small animals. Take care that you cut only the sharp pointed tip. You might want to have an anticoagulant handy to stop any accidental bleeding. Keep your pet's cage clean so that your pet's nails are less likely to cause an infection of the wounds. Including a variety of foods in your rat's diet, especially fruits and vegetables, seems to help prevent this condition, as does a low-protein diet.

GROOMING

A rat's skin secretes oils that the rat distributes by licking and grooming itself. This gives the coat a glossy shine. Proper nutrition is needed for healthy skin and coat. Poor appearance of the skin and coat is often a warning that something might be wrong.

You might wish to clean your rat if it gets dirty from lying on damp shavings or if its coat gets stained. You can do so with a mild baby or cat shampoo. Support your pet's forequarters and let it stand up in a sink. Use lukewarm water. Be sure to completely rinse your rat. It is best to use a towel to dry your rat; improper use of a hair dryer can cause burns on its sensitive skin. Many rats enjoy being brushed. You can use a soft toothbrush to brush your rat. Don't press down, though; use light strokes.

INJURIES

You can help prevent injuring your rat by handling it properly. Pick it up gently without squeezing it. If you let others hold or play with your rat, show them how to do so. Even though your rat is extremely agile and a good climber, you must still be careful if you let it climb on any high objects. A fall could cause a broken bone or internal injuries. Rats are smart and can sense the edge of a table and will not topple off. If your pet rides around on your shoulder, you must see to it that it remains securely on your shoulder. A rat has excellent senses and will hold on strongly, but you must be careful not to cause it to fall. If your pet does fall and appears injured, you might need to have it X-rayed for a fractured limb or spine.

Foot injuries, such as a swollen foot or loss of a toenail, might be caused by the cage or self-mutilation. Prevention includes making sure the bedding covers

A very old rat, rather infirm and lethargic.

the wire floor of the cage. Your rat might bleed from an injured toenail, but it will usually heal without complication.

OLD RATS

A pet rat lives an average of three years, although there are reports of pet rats living for five years. Rats decline into old age before they die. Old rats lose weight, their bones become more prominent, and they feel frail to the touch. Their fur becomes thinner and fluffier. Because they groom themselves less, their coat aren't as lustrous. The coats of old albino rats, especially males, tend to become coarse and yellow. An old rat isn't as active and will be content to just sit alongside you and have its back scratched.

Old rats' senses are less keen, and they might become deaf or have diminished eyesight. Some old rats can become lame. You should check your pet's front teeth and make sure they are still meeting properly. An elderly pet is less resistant to disease, so practice preventive health care by keeping its cage clean. If you think your old rat might be suffering, you can take it to a veterinarian and have it painlessly put to sleep.

TRAVEL AND VACATION

A rat likes to go places, and it can be fun to bring your pet for a visit with friends, relatives, or to school for show and tell. You can use a special carrying cage, made for transporting small animals on airplanes or going to the veterinarian. These cages are made of plastic and are lightweight. They usually have a handle and are easily carried. You can also use your rat's regular cage; but if it is a wire-frame cage, you should partially cover it with a cloth. This will help your rat to feel less vulnerable and exposed, and also protect it from drafts. Be sure to protect your rat from direct sunlight.

You can also take your pet with you when you go on your vacation. A plastic or wooden carrying cage is ideal for traveling. Be sure your pet gets a nesting box. Your must protect your rat from direct sunlight and drafts when traveling. If you leave the cage in the shade in the car, make sure that it will still be in the shade later in the day.

Most gravity-fed water bottles do not work in moving vehicles. You can offer water to your rat when it is awake or set up the bottle only when the car has stopped moving. Professional shippers provide small animals with pieces of apples or potatoes for moisture. You can also do this.

If the temperature is going to be very warm at your vacation site (say, hotter than 80°F), you should not take your pet. You can leave your pet rat unattended for up to a week while you go on vacation. You should provide your rat with *two* water bottles. Set up the water bottles away from the food in case they leak. Using a large dish that cannot be tipped over, give your rat enough dry food for each day that you will be gone. It is also a good idea to provide your rat with extra food, such as honey-coated bird seed sticks. Do not leave any moist foods in the cage because they could spoil. If you are going to be gone longer than a week, you should arrange for a friend or relative to take care of your rat. Then your rat can have fresh food and water, and a clean cage.

FANCY RAT CLUBS

American Fancy Rat and
Mouse Association
9230 64th Street
Riverside, CA 92509

American Rat, Mouse and
Hamster Society
c/o Sandy Ramey
9370 Adlai Road
Lakeside, CA 92040